Be A Big Fish

Paco Muro

newcelona.com

Be A Big Fish

Paco Muro

Translated from the original in spanish
"El pez que no quiso evolucionar"

Versión P.O.D. - 1a Edición - Febrero 2013

ISBN: 978-84-935593-3-5

TABLE OF CONTENTS

PART ONE

Eight Contemporary Tales

CHAPTER . 01

"If You Don't Go There ...
Then You Haven't Been!"

"My last three months' sales have been lousy!" complained Tom, one of the company sales reps.

He was talking to his old friend, Sergio, a veteran salesman. For years, they'd been meeting up once a month at the pub, and while they enjoyed a beer, Tom would tell Sergio the thousand-and-one problems he was having, and how difficult everything was getting. Sergio, who was an old hand, waited for the second round to be served, and asked him:

"Do you know that article, "*If you don't go there… then you haven't been*!"?

"Which one? No… it doesn't ring any bells. Why do you ask?"

"I am going to send it to you - I think you need it. David, our general manager, gave it to us at our last congress. It was the most photocopied article of the year, last year. Not long ago, the director of a finance company told me that that loads of his branch managers keep it locked away in their safe, like some sort of personal treasure! I'll send it to you this afternoon, and next month, when we meet, you can tell me what you think."

That same afternoon Sergio, reliable as ever, sent over a copy of the article, which had been published in a well-known financial Sunday newspaper, a few months earlier.

Salesmen are tempted to find countless excuses when it comes to justifying bad sales results. So much so, in fact, that they often fall into the trap of believing their own facile excuses. Then their performance begins to slow down and, almost without realising, it becomes a self-fulfilling prophecy; at which point the wind-mills really do turn into giants.

Everywhere, we hear voices claiming that it's a tough market, competition is tough, the sector's going through a rough patch, our prices are no good, we take too long to get back to clients, our sales area is too large, we're doing too much work, we don't have time for anything... And, quite possibly, most of these objections are true.

So, what's the solution? How can we break this vicious circle that undermines sales peoples' morale and has a negative impact on their results?

* * *

Every time we capture a new client,
it means some other naive sales rep
has lost one of their own "captive clients."

* * *

The answer: do what you normally do. Do what a sales rep is meant to do, the whole point of their job: visit, visit, visit!

The thing is that with all these excuses and all this neglect, we stop visiting clients that we should be visiting. We stop making the phone calls that we should be making; the pace drops, the tone fades, and we lose the motivation to sell.

Most clients stop working with suppliers because they have been "dropped" by them. We take captive clients for granted and we stop visiting them, until we discover that they weren't in fact "captive", after all.

We just need to remember that, every time we capture a new client, it means some other naive sales rep has lost one of their own captive clients.

Now, IT, telemarketing, the web, CRM, and so forth, are all good things, and they make great back-up tools. But selling - real selling - is done face-to-face, by listening and seizing opportunities as they arise, on the spot. This is because behind every client there is a person, with individual quirks and wishes. If we forget to deal with the person, we

9

deserve to lose the client.

In the company I manage, we often say: "If you don't go there … then you haven't been. If you don't phone … then you haven't phoned."

* * *
Behind each client there is a person,
with individual quirks and wishes.
If we forget to deal with the person, we deserve to lose the client.
* * *

This should serve to remind us that it doesn't matter what the market is like, or what product we want to cover: what we have to do is visit. Visit, go there, phone. Because if you don't go … you haven't been - and if you haven't been, you most certainly haven't seized any opportunities, generated any business, sold the product image, been given any introductions or references, found out about any future alterations which may affect you, taken any of those unexpected orders that can turn up when you visit somewhere… and a long list of other good things that happen to salespeople who do visit and phone.

It's always good to keep in mind that, in sales, there is such a thing as good luck - but it has to catch you visiting! Is the current market difficult? Then, go and visit! Is competition tough? Then, go and visit even more! Is there giant meteorite heading towards earth and it could be the end of the world as we know it…? Go and visit - just in case!.

Everything else is secondary. If you go there, you may come away with an order - or maybe not. But if you don't go there…

Of course the market seems tough, and of course competition is strong! All the excuses that can be devised by the hopeless, lazy salesman inside us all will appear before you, a thousand-fold.

Fortunately, we also carry inside us an energy-driven professional, who enjoys a challenge, delights in setting goals, likes direct contact with other people, and loves to experience the freedom of being salesperson. This is the kind of salesperson who savours every achievement, sticks to the job like a hound on the scent, and who, whenever he meets a client who treats him like dirt, instead of feeling sorry for himself thinks: "Just you watch! I'll get my own revenge by selling you something!"

This true professional is the one we need to arouse when the venom of mediocrity starts to rise within us.

The best way to do this is by visiting, and visiting yet again. Visits are the very essence of sales, the field of action for a salesperson; it is the moment of truth, where we go for all or nothing, where we make or break a deal. This is when you can feel that sales adrenaline, fueling the spirit of the professional salesperson.

Of course, it all needs to be thought out, planned and prepared - but it has to be based on a visit! And if your visit is of a high standard because of your great sales technique as well as good organization, then better still! There are many who will say: "Yes, but I need more time to prepare", or, "yes, but I need training", "yes, but we don't have enough support, the brochure is out of date"... Yes, but... yes, but... yes, but....!

Meanwhile, the hours, days and weeks go by, and you still haven't "been there"!

* * *

This is when you can feel that sales adrenaline fueling the spirit
of the professional salesperson.

* * *

So, while you're busy thinking about it, and while someone tries to update the brochures, while you're waiting for proper training, (which is always a good healthy option for a professional), and even when the Greek God of Finance decides to fill

11

the market with eager clients phoning you and willing to spend huge amounts of money without any encouragement at all….

… GO AND VISIT!

Because if you don't go there, let's face it: you haven't been!

Sergio couldn't wait to see Tom and ask him how he felt after reading the article. He ordered a couple of beers and, just before they got served, his friend arrived. Tom leaned on the bar and said, with a smile:

"You're a ….! I almost phoned you, several times, just to tell you what I thought. But then, when my ego had cooled down, I decided to channel the energy away from my anger and onto myself - and it transformed itself into courage. I've been making more calls than ever, I've been visiting non-stop, and the most annoying thing is, I've hooked more new business this month than in the entire past year! I admit, you were right - thanks for sending me the article. This round's on me!"

"Good for you!", replied Sergio. "The same thing happened to me when my boss handed out the article to all of us in the Projects Department. At first I was furious, but a couple of days later I wasn't hearing a single complaint from anyone, and we were all "going there" like crazy."

"Well, these things happen. By the way, Sergio, where did you park your car?"

"Oh, five blocks away… I saw a slot and went for it - it's hopeless around here lately."

"Gotcha!" cried Tom. "You pay for the next round."

"What? Why?"

"Because you're supposed to be the one teaching lessons, yet you're the first one to fall by the wayside! You can apply that article to other things besides selling, you know: it's also for people who don't "go there" in life, because it's easier to make yourself comfortable and make up excuses than to move. I'm applying it to everything now, and, for example, I realized that the only people who manage to park right by the door are the ones who come right up to the door. Guess where I left the car today?"

"Right by the door? Really? Now, that is luck!"

"Yes – it's the luck of someone who actually "goes there". Because now, I try. I come right up to the door, just in case - and I get a slot more often that you would think. Come on, pay up and learn from the Master..."

Sergio was quite happy to pay for the drinks.

A few minutes later, a pair of good-looking young women walked into the pub, and Tom remarked:

"Wonder who the lucky guys are who get to go out with those two stunners, eh?

They sat there in silence. Then they suddenly looked at each other, shrugged, and said, at the same time:

"If we don't go there.... we shan't have been!"

They grabbed their beer glasses, got up, and walked over to have a word with the two girls.

Who cares what happened next!

CHAPTER . 02

Row!

"Each man to his oar!"

With these words David Borj, General Manager of a distribution factory, closed the last quarterly monitoring meeting with his team:

"You and your Norwegian stories", said Sergio as they left the meeting. Sergio was one of the sales reps, and he enjoyed the way David solved disputes. You could tell he was Scandinavian, with all the expressions and explanations that never failed to surprise his staff.

The subject arose when he informed his team that he had decided to alter the product plan in order to improve the placement strategy. This news led to a certain amount of tension and an avalanche of complaints and problems from all areas.

David tried to talk to everyone, and was prepared to listen to their input but, seeing that he was clearly making no headway, he stopped the discussion and told them a story that his grandfather had told to his father, and which his father had told to him.

When the story was over, he waited for a response, but nobody said anything. They therefore decided that, at the next meeting, if anyone wished to contribute an idea, they should do so according to the new rules they had learned from the story. As everyone stood up to leave, he called out the "oar" phrase as a farewell cry.

Here is the story, as he told it to them:

Olaf, the experienced captain of a Viking ship, was given the crucial mission of stocking up with provisions for the Great Village, before the bad weather cut them off for the winter.

The village was isolated both by land and sea for months on end, until the melt waters enabled the trade routes to open up once again. This meant it was the most important journey each autumn. This year, the challenge was even greater, as the ancient port of Nervik, where they had gone for centuries to stock up on supplies, had been devastated by fierce hordes from the East.

The only other option for purchasing stocks was Reyka, a town that lay a several days' hard voyage away. To get there, they had to sail into the long Nork fjord, and travel several miles upstream, along one of the rivers. The strong current made sailing extremely dangerous, with turbulent waters, treacherous whirlpools and shores edged with hundreds of almost invisible rocks that were hard to avoid. The journey was going to be dangerous, and Olaf knew very well that he would only be able to reach his goal by using his skill and bravery. But he had no option: it was a case of the tribe's survival.

When he saw they were getting close to their destination, he gave his instructions to the crew:

"My brave Vikings, we are approaching the most difficult part of our mission. We are entering the fjord close to the north shore, avoiding the rocks. Half a mile further up, we will head for the centre of the fjord to avoid the side currents. The lookout will warn us of any eddies that might be forming ahead of us, so we can try to avoid them. After this, we will push against the outflow and head upriver at full speed. Once we are beyond the outflow, the rest should be easy, as the waters are calmer upstream, and deep enough for us to row without problems."

After hearing these words, Eric, one of the most experienced sailors on board, set down his oar and stood up to give his opinion:

"Olaf, I don't agree with your plan. I understand there are lots of rocks, and it will be very dangerous. What's more, you cannot always can see the eddies in time, and in the final stretch the current is very strong and will be difficult to sail against, even with the wind in our

15

favour and rowing with all our might. This boat is old and the mast is not reliable – it may not withstand the pressure it will have to bear."

The captain did not like such negative criticism. For a second he nearly got his whip out to enforce his orders, but Erik was one of his best men and he thought others might share the man's opinion.

He knew his plan was risky, but the mission was crucial. It was essential for everyone to give their best effort. When so much is at stake, you cannot risk everything just because you refuse to listen to alternatives.
He was not entirely convinced that his own decisions were right, so any other solution would be welcome. If they didn't get to Reyka quickly and stock up on provisions, many of his people would die that winter. It was also urgent to make a quick decision, as the tide would turn very shortly and then it would be impossible to undertake the voyage at all.

There was too much at risk to just blunder ahead because he was not able to analyze the alternatives. So, finally, he decided to control his anger and show everyone he was willing to listen to experienced sailors:

"Very well. I know this spot, and its difficulties, and I realize that my plan is not perfect. I will take that responsibility. In the past I have suffered at the hands of stupid captains who were too blinded by their own vanity and pride to admit different opinions, and more than once I have ended up shipwrecked as a result. So, my good Eric, I have told you my plan, and now I am willing to listen to yours. Have you got an alternative plan for reaching our goal on time?"

The sailor, who so far had only mentioned obstacles and problems, sat thinking, while the rest of his friends waited to hear his answer. Seeing the expectant look on their faces, he said:

"Above all, I would like to make it clear that even if I had a plan, I wouldn't want to be made responsible for making such a delicate decision".

"Don't worry," interrupted Olaf. "The final decision will be mine and, therefore, so will the responsibility. All I ask is that, as you have raised questions and expressed doubts and concerns, you propose a solution for carrying out this mission with a greater chance of success. Seeing mistakes and faults in other people's idea is easy – anyone can do that. Criticizing what already exists is of no use - but providing intelligent options for improving the original idea, is. Well, I'll repeat my question: do you have a better alternative?"

After a moment's silence, Eric decided to talk, and tell them his conclusions:

"Really, I can't come up with any other less dangerous route. I admit that I don't know these waters that well, so I don't know how to go about this more safely".

* * *

It is easy to see other people's mistakes.
The useful thing is not to criticize what's already there,
but to support or give intelligent alternatives
to improve the original idea.

* * *

"Well, Eric", the captain replied with his usual mildness, "in that case, carry on thinking of possible solutions and if you come up with a better alternative don't hesitate to tell us straight away. I will give you my full attention".

But in the meantime: SHUT UP AND ROW WITH ALL YOUR MIGHT, FOR ODIN´S SAKE!

Olaf and the expedition finally did reach Reyka. They loaded up their provisions and the Great Village survived yet another hard winter. The captain's decision-making skill and the combined strength of every member of the crew had made it possible.

***

If you don't have a better alternative, keep thinking.
But in the meantime… keep rowing!

***

CHAPTER . 03

"What If They Get Unmotivated And Stay?"

David received a phone call from the Managing Director of one of the companies he had been providing with advisory services. The MD was concerned, because his company was going through an increasing turnover of qualified professional staff. In fact, he suspected that some of his key professionals were thinking of leaving the company.

Although he had analyzed this situation in depth, he could not figure out why it was happening. The salaries of key members of staff had been reviewed not long ago and were above average for the sector. Despite this, he had not managed to solve the problem. He was worried it would get out of hand.

He therefore decided to consult David, considering him to be a trustworthy professional, with whom from time to time he liked to share his ideas and concerns. He had always believed that someone who was unaware of a problem would see the solution more clearly than someone who was immersed in it.

"David, I'm in a very awkward situation. I'm losing the people I most need to manage the company. Some have gone already, and I'm afraid more will soon be leaving; these people are essential for achieving our company goals.

Perhaps if I insisted on a salary review it might be easier to hold onto them. I don't know what to do. I fear they may become unmotivated and leave."

"Eugenio, I think you're underestimating the problem. From what you have told me, things are worse than you imagine."

"Worse? I'm telling you, I may lose some of my key people!"

"Yes, but retaining them would not solve the problem. It would be worse if they became unmotivated and stayed. It would be just like not having them, and it would cost you a fortune! Enthusiasm fuels talent. Without it, the knowledge, experience and intelligence of your personnel will produce results that are well below their potential, and might even stop altogether."

* * *
Enthusiasm fuels talent.
Without it, the knowledge, experience and intelligence
of personnel works well below potential.
* * *

"I hadn't thought of that! The situation is really bad. I need them to stay, but I also need them to be enthusiastic and to feel satisfied with themselves and with the company. Otherwise, they'll influence the rest of the staff and won't do their best. This is crucial: our goals are vital for the future of the company."

Eugenio decided to switch focus, and asked David to help him design a specific plan of action to recover the enthusiasm of his best people and ensure that they recovered their pride and sense of belonging. To start with, he wanted to agree with his advisor about the money involved.

"How much is this going to cost, David?"

"I can see you still don't get it. It isn't a question of money, but VALUE."

"I don't follow you. What do you mean, value? Don't you think money has value?"

"Yes - especially when you haven't got any. But that's not the case here. Your people's salaries are fine. You won't solve motivational problems with money. You need something greater than that, something much more highly prized by that level of professional."

"What would that be? How much does it cost?"

David smiled gently at Eugenio and, after a few seconds, replied:

"What you need is imagination. It's harder than you think, because it's not a matter of having, but of wanting. We have to make people feel wanted, valued; we want them to feel that this company adds value to their professional and personal life."

* * *

We have to make people feel wanted, valued;
we want them to feel that this company adds value
to their professional and personal life.

* * *

Eugenio had been focusing on results, figures and decisions for too long, and he had lost touch with the everyday reality of human beings at work.

So he decided to trust his advisor. He was prepared to learn another lesson about business life. After studying the individual needs of each man and woman involved, different wishes and requirements became apparent. It was clear that some of those in charge, who had been working in the company for a long time, needed a change of department in order to face new challenges and recover their lost enthusiasm. Others needed to adjust their working hours so they could organize their personal life better. For the latter group, a flexible system was set up that would help everyone to adapt their work schedule to their personal life.

They also looked for ways of making things easier for staff with school-age children. Other people only wanted some recognition and appreciation of their work and achievements.

He had been so blinded by his obsession with results, he had almost forgotten the key to obtaining them: people.

A top-level management and people skills training program was put together to improve managers' style. This helped them each to find the emotional balance required in order to trigger verve and determination, which they then passed on to their team. Very soon the company recovered its positive energy and, to Eugenio´s surprise, some of the "runaways" even came back.

"David, my friend, I was so wrong! I never realized how important it is to take care of people. I was so blinded by my obsession with results I almost forgot the key to obtaining them: people. Now I understand that dealing with staff's emotional needs is part of how a company makes its people feel valued."

For key professionals, value is not based on money, but on concrete facts that prove that the company and its managers are able to make their employees feel respected and appreciated. So, issues like flexibility or reconciling work and family life are not just social dialogue: they are real, motivating management tools, and real leadership goals. Only this way will we be able to retain the enthusiasm of our best people, and pass it on to others.

CHAPTER . 04

Don´T Tell Me. Show Me!

Hugh was an experienced professional employee who lost his job after the company he worked for decided to streamline.

He started looking for work and after a number of attempts, he realized that it wasn't going to be as easy as he had thought. He received an unattractive offer from a company with no clear project. They asked him if he would be prepared to travel abroad and if he would take on a short-term project.

Then in the end, he found something with a future and a certain degree of stability. David's company, which had a great reputation in terms of both service and staff quality, was looking for experienced people to join its Sales Department.

The position seemed promising, but he had to start from scratch, as he didn't know the sector, the products, or the new company's way of doing things. He started with a good salary, although it was significantly lower than his previous one.

After he had been with company for a few months, during which time he hadn't negotiated any sales, he went to see the director.

"I'm very happy in the company," he told him, "but, to be honest, David, I have to say my salary is rather low. I like the work, I know I am going to do it well and in sales terms I know I'm going to be able to attract clients and develop projects. I do understand that there are commissions on results, but we all know that until I learn, and my work produces some results, it's going to take me a while to make enough money. Don't forget that I used to earn a lot more."

David was not surprised by the newcomer's reaction. In fact, he knew he had recruited a top-level employee, with plenty of potential, and he considered it perfectly normal for him to express his concerns.

* * *

If you prove the potential that you claim you have with actual results, everything will fall into place: your income, your performance and the company's equilibrium.
* * *

So he asked him:
"Are you saying that you need your previous salary in order to maintain the lifestyle to which you are accustomed, or that you consider that you're "worth" that salary as an employee in this business?"

Hugh was taken aback. The truth was, he had based his calculations on his own habits and personal needs, and he hadn't considered whether or not his current contribution was consistent with that figure. However, he believed in himself and in his potential progress in this new line of business, so he replied:

"I suppose the figure matches my personal needs, but I honestly believe it's what I should be earning."

David merely replied:

"Well, if that's the case, everything will be fine. Here, we have a wage system that sets a decent basic fixed salary, with very good chances of increasing the variable wage. Working hard and well, you could manage to double your starting salary, which would make it even higher than the figure you mentioned. Some people have managed to do that. If you learn fast, work well and your results prove all the potential you say you have – which I believe - then everything will fall into place: your income, your performance and the company's equilibrium.

So, as far as I'm concerned, I will have no problem paying you more if you earn it. What's more, I recruited you in the expectation that you *will* earn it. Let's not discuss you salary again. Professional worth

24

is not something you talk about – it's something you prove.-"

* * *

Professional worth is not something you talk about
– it's something you prove.
What people do is a more reliable guide than what they say.
* * *

David added:

"If you believe that that is your correct salary level, go ahead. Don't *tell* me what you are worth, simply *make yourself worth it*! Deserve the best and you'll get it. I learned a long time ago that, when judging people, what they do is a more reliable guide than what they say. All managers need valuable people who produce solid results; it's the best way to ensure you get what you want. If you prove what you are really worth, Hugh, you can count on me being the first person to make sure that you are happy, motivated and involved in the company.

* * *

All directors need valuable people who provide solid results.
Show what you are worth and you will get what you deserve.
* * *

CHAPTER . 05

What'S So Great About Having A Boss?

"Who would have told me that one day I'd be saying 'It's great to have a boss'…" said David.

He was at a sector association dinner and was sharing a table with Helena, a colleague from another company who was also the general manager of her firm. The conversation was pleasant and the company appropriate for telling a few personal stories. So he openly discussed one or two conclusions he had come to, based on his own experience.

"A few years ago, when I was an ordinary member of staff, I was only concerned about my own area of work. It was very easy to question the decisions sent down from above while, in the meantime, all I had to do was do enough to stand out from the crowd. I could even suggest new ideas and alternatives, because I knew that in the end, of course, someone else would be made responsible for them.

Later on, I got promoted to a middle-management position. My interest in taking on work must have been noticed, because I replaced the person in charge of my area after he left. In this job the difference was that I now had to "make people do things". My work consisted of conveying decisions to my team. My scope for changing things was narrow, and my decisions were only short-range. They weren't strategic decisions and, once again, I felt free from heavier responsibilities.

In the end, it was others who made the decision to go one way or another, to launch a certain product, create goals, or to diversify... And I was still able to question what was decided by those higher up."

Helena was glad to hear her friend's remarks. She somehow identified with a number of the things he was saying.

"It always seemed like the guys at the top didn't do anything, don't you think?" she asked. "We were the ones who did all the work. At least that's what it felt like. And I used to rather envy the role of the General Director. A General and a Director at the same time! A Director with the power of a General – it had to be the best thing ever!"

"Yes, I used to think that too," agreed David. "Then I started climbing up the professional ladder. Each time I had more scope to express my opinion, but I always had someone above me who paved the way. When later, I got to the so-called "top", I had a huge surprise. To start with, being General Director wasn't what I thought. A better description would be "Director, in General", in other words, a director of pretty much everything".

"Too right," agreed Helena. "The basic difference is that, as a General Director, everything affects you directly. I used to be only worried about my own area, my own territory. The rest of the company was important, but what happened in other departments wasn't *my* problem – it was up to whoever was in charge of that area. My only involvement was to complain if my area was affected or perhaps suggesting ways to improve things. But it was up to them whether they agreed or not.

I always felt involved in the company, but you couldn't help feeling your own area was your priority. Now, as a General Director, the smallest issue affects you, regardless of who is going to resolve it. The results of every Department in the company are our direct responsibility."

"What's more," added David, "if you want to have a good working environment, you need to share the credit for the successes, and deal with all the failures yourself. Nowadays, hardly anybody congratulates you, even when you've managed to make improvements for the company, or when you've saved it from a crisis by making the right personal decision in time. That's no big deal. As far as everyone else is concerned, it's your job to get it right – that's why you get a big fat paycheck!"

"And worst of all, you don't have a boss to blame!"

David burst out laughing. At last he could talk to someone who understood and shared the private concerns shared by most senior managers. When he had stopped laughing, he added:

"You can no longer say 'I just did what I was told' or 'I told you that wouldn't work' – all those things that free you from any moral blame. Now, if you get it wrong it might have serious consequences: one of your mistakes could cause a huge loss to the company. We have to find the balance among all the work performed by the entire company, in order to have a successful and coordinated team. We constantly have to foresee the future, make blindfold decisions based on a gut instinct for what the best thing is for tomorrow and, on the basis of that alone, we have to establish what has to be done today in order to reach that future in the best possible conditions. And we have to just get on with it, with no crystal ball and no guarantees..."

"And fully aware that a lot of people won't understand the decisions we make, and that we'll be criticized. So, you end up accepting that you can't make everybody happy."

"That's right. And if everything turns out OK, very few people, if any, will acknowledge the skill of whichever boss had to make the tough decision. The credit will go to everyone, because it the decision was implemented by managers and employees alike. There is no thought for the person took the actual risk of deciding what had to be done."

"In any case, David, when that "tomorrow" eventually comes, senior managers are already focusing on "the day after tomorrow", or other new things that pop up that nobody else knows about - and never will know about. Our role is to convey a feeling of safety and calm. We have to keep the worries to ourselves, to avoid unnecessary tension in the company."

"No, the big fat paycheck is not just for fun. I knew there had to be something they weren't telling me about when I became a senior manager. Nowadays, nothing's free in business, so there's a reason that senior managers' salaries are being so high. The main difference is that, as a General Director, everything affects you directly, and the worst of it is that you can't pass the problem on to someone else."

"We all know there's always some wise guy out there who knows better - we were once a bit like that. He or she will say, quite rightly, that it might have been a lot better done in a different way, and how come we're so dumb. I say "quite rightly", because we may well agree with them. But the trouble is that those voices are always heard *after* the event, when they can see the results and the new facts right in front of them."

"Any darn fool can do that, Helena! It's easy to bet on a winner after the race. What I want to know is, how come we don't hear any of those voices when we're asking people for ideas, solutions and commitment? Where are they when we need someone who is brave enough to risk their job by making a strategic decision?"

"They're working away, and waiting," she replied, "because it's a lot more comfortable having a boss do the choosing, and to suffer the consequences of their decisions. All in all, experience ends up teaching you that having a boss is a pretty cushy job! And if on top of all that, he or she is a nice person, a good professional and a hard worker - what could be better?"

"That's why I wish that the staff and technicians in charge of different areas, as well as all the middle-managers, would try to be a bit more understanding," said David. "They should cooperate with their boss, and particularly with their principal ally, the general manager. They might not think so, but there is no more involved and enthusiastic member of staff than their own boss when it comes to seeing them obtain the best results."

"The least that qualified professionals should be expected to do, when facing any decision that comes from the top - regardless of whether they understand it or it is clear to them - is to ask a few questions before judging it. Most of the time, there is a reason for decisions. And if the explanation is still unconvincing, they should bear in mind that, after making a decision, we senior managers will always welcome and consider any valuable contribution from a member of the team who can suggest a better alternative."

* * *

You might not think so, but there is no more involved and enthusiastic member of staff than your own boss when it comes to seeing you obtain the best results.

* * *

"When in doubt, if there is nothing to prove a decision is no good, it's best to support it. In the end, it's the senior manager who's responsible for what's been decided, and one should assume that they know what they're doing."

"I'm glad to see I'm not the only one who thinks all this! I feel the same", said Helena. "I admit that I've been unfair to some of the bosses I've had in the past - those who did the right thing - because I never made the effort to understand them. I thought it was up to them to make themselves understood, as if it were their duty to be perfect. Now I've learned how 'great' it is to have a boss."
"That's why it was a good thing that we did tell one or two of them to get lost - the ones that didn't deserve our hard work."

"Right!"

* * *

Good bosses will always appreciate a better alternative proposed by someone else, and will consider it an added value.

* * *

CHAPTER . 06

The Leadership Values Of The Wizard Of Oz

The Financial Director of the company, Marina, had rented a classic movie to watch with her daughter. She had seen "The Wizard of Oz" several times - it was one of her favourite films. That's why, although she was already a successful executive in a multinational company, she still felt very excited about the film and wanted to share it with her little girl.

But, this time, Marina was surprised to see something in the film she had never noticed before. The following day, at lunch, she discussed what she had seen with David.

"I watched "The Wizard of Oz" with my daughter yesterday, and this time I saw some leadership ideas that I had never noticed before. Does that sound silly?"

"Not at all," replied David. "Did you know that it's not only an extraordinary story, and a classic, but that it has a sub-plot containing the basic features of leadership values? It might be because, when he wrote the book, Frank Baum still wasn't a proper author, but a company sales rep. He may have got his inspiration from some of the things he saw and experienced in the company he worked for."

"I didn't know that. I thought he'd always been a writer."

"No, that came later. Look carefully at the three characters that accompany Dorothy. They go to see the wizard to ask him for something: the Tin Man wanted a heart, so he could feel emotions; the Scarecrow wanted a brain so he could think with intelligence; and the Lion wanted courage so he could cope with difficult situations. All these are key features of management:

The heart is the source of passion: it can move mountains and people's own will. It stands for the emotional side of staff management and project management. A good manager is one who firmly believes in a project and likes to convey this to others. He is the kind who backs his own team, and lets his team know it. Our heart helps us to treat other people like human beings, not like machines or "resources". The heart makes us appreciate our team. All the appreciation and dedication you gives to your collaborators is returned as loyalty, enthusiasm and complete involvement.

Intelligence, thought and reflection are essential features of a good executive. He has to base his decisions on reasoned judgements, has to manage by "using his head", and showing there is a coherent criteria for all his actions.

The brain should give shape to our intuition. It is the key to method, planning, preparation, reflection and all the conscious features that have to be cultivated and developed by every executive in order to be a successful manager, in other words, to make the team that he manages achieve success.

* * *

All the appreciation and dedication you gives to your collaborators is returned as loyalty, enthusiasm and complete involvement.

* * *

And last, but not least, there is **courage**, the piece that completes the set. Without courage we can't cope with decisions, challenges, changes, risks, mistakes, developments, or anything else. Everything the heart desires and the brain works out and prepares, falls apart if we don't have the courage to make it happen.

Some people have the courage to make decisions and changes when things are going wrong. This is a degree of courage unknown to many. But the highest level of courage, the one that only a few people ever achieve and maintain, is the courage to change things when everything is going well. The courage to make decisions today that will help us to foresee the changes of tomorrow.

This kind of courage is special, because it is quite likely that any action taken today will not be understood by the majority, and will be questioned by many. It's not easy to make changes when things are going well. Even the best leaders are fully aware that this kind of action is undertaken without any guarantee of ultimate success."

* * *

The highest level of courage is the courage to change things
when everything is going well.

* * *

"What a pity that these three basic management skills are not encouraged more, and even more strictly required" said Marina. "If a manager is weak in any one of those areas, he or she should be removed from the job as soon as possible, and be given appropriate training to regain those missing skills. If the manager regains them, then welcome back: if not, he or she should stay where his or her talents can be applied, but should not be allowed to manage the professional fate of a company and its staff."

"I couldn't agree more. Managing, and managing people, in particular, is not a game. It's a highly professional specialty that doesn't allow for half-measures. The consequences of any mistake are extremely serious, and the entire company may suffer. To be a manger, you need to have returned from the Land of Oz, not be on your way there... The success of a company is not a lottery; it depends on the correct, professional work of people who deserve to be in management positions, as well as on the efforts of efficiently-led co-workers."

"You are so right! Here, let me get you a coffee..."

CHAPTER . 07

The Tale Of Dunnit And Issjust

"Do you have the details of your first quarter sales that I asked you to prepare?" David asked Hugh, who was responsible for the product. He was one of the people who had joined the company a long time ago, and he was a good friend.

"Sorry, not yet," replied Hugh. "I've been working on the new reference numbers. I haven't had time… it's just that being new and all that…"

"Hugh, you know I'm your friend, and it worries me to see you always looking so overwhelmed. If you could just try to be Dunnit, you would be a lot happier - and you'd feel more worthwhile if you were achieving something."

"Be a what? I'm sorry, I didn't understand..."

"Don't worry. Let me tell you a story that changed my life", offered David.

"My mother told it to me and it helped me to start doing things in a different way. It's no exaggeration to say that it has been one of the key factors of my success. I mean that in the sense that I enjoy life, I'm very happy with what I am and what I do, with my profession, my family and with myself."

"Another Viking story?"

"No - my mother's Spanish! It's my Dad who's from Norway," David answered, smiling.

"In that case, I guess you'll have to tell me the story!"

"Come on. It'll only take five minutes."

They stopped off at the hot drinks machine and sat down at a round table next to a meeting room. While the coffees were cooling down, David started to tell Hugh the story:

"There were once two friends, who, when they turned 18, decided to go to work in a new factory that had recently built in a nearby village.

From day one, both of them did their utmost, but soon they could see big differences in their style of working and their career paths. While one lad, Dunnit, was getting recognition from his boss, the other, Issjust, was convinced that his boss didn't trust him or believe in him, for some unknown reason.

"I don't know, Dunnit, but I don't think they like me. I do what I can, I try to be useful, but I just don't connect with my boss somehow. There's no chemistry between us."

"I'm sorry to hear that," said Dunnit. "I'm doing really well. I feel very comfortable here and just today the director told me that I am going to be promoted to foreman."

"You're really lucky!" sighed Issjust. "That kind of thing never happens to me. We're the same age, we've studied the same things, we have the same amount of experience, we're both keen to do things. I don't understand it..."

"Well mate, maybe you should talk to your boss, or with the manager. They might be able to explain if there's something you haven't noticed," advised Dunnit.

The next day, Issjust, spoke to the Area Manager and told him about his concerns and worries. The boss, whose name was Emilio, thought carefully about how to help the young man understand why he wasn't making any progress. He liked the lad, so he promised to help him, and asked him to wait a few days while he though about what to do.

The following week, first thing in the morning, Emilio called both friends and said to them:

"I need you to clear up and put away all the maintenance material for these machines. You can do Warehouse nº 1, and you do nº 2. This afternoon before you leave, I want to see you both to find out how you got on. Any questions?"

"Any particular criteria?" enquired Dunnit.

"However you think best, but it needs to be practical and easy," replied Emilio.

That said, Dunnit left to start on the job.
When they were alone, the boss looked at the other young man, who was standing there, quiet and thoughtful.

"Anything you want to say?" he asked.

"Well, it's just that I think it will be difficult to tidy up properly. There is always someone using something. And then there are quite a few bits that are of no use, but we still keep them."

"You do what you think is best and tell me about it later."

"Yes, but, it's just that we won't be able to classify everything, and also they won't fit in the same cupboard."

"Are you sure? Do you know if that's the case, or are you just supposing?"

"No, I'm not sure, but it *is* going to be complicated…"

"In that case go ahead and tell me all about it this afternoon."

At the end of the day Issjust walked into Emilio´s office. He was stressed-out and depressed. He said:

"I've been working on it, but I not making much progress. It's just that I started going round the warehouse looking for all the tools that weren't in their place, and it was a nightmare. Even so, I went to the cupboards to decide how to divide up the space and it was impossible, because they were full of rags and old material. It's just that, we need to throw them away first, in order to see how much space is left."

"OK, do that tomorrow."

"Yes. It's just that there are too many, and I don't think they'll fit in the skip outside."

"You don't think they'll fit, or they definitely don't fit?"

"Well, I don't think they'll fit..."

"Have you been to look at the skip?"

"Yes. Well, no. It's just that the other day there was a lot going on and all the packaging had been thrown into it, and it must be full by now."

"Are you sure?"

"No, not entirely. But I haven't had time to go and see it. It's just that I received a call from the warehouse to go and see something, and one thing led to another and I couldn't go and check…"

Emilio didn't say anything. As he caught sight of Dunnit coming towards them, he decided to wait. When Dunnit caught up with them, Emilio asked:

"Well, how did it go with the tools?"

"Done it. It's all ready."

"Everything?"

"Yes. It took me a bit longer, because I took advantage of it to get rid of all the old material and empty the cupboards, and I left them ready for more things."

"And, did you manage to throw everything away?"

"Yes, although I needed another skip because ours was almost full. Anyway, I mentioned it to the floor supervisor, and he told me that they needed another one too, so I went ahead and ordered one."

"Well done! Did you find out when it'll be in place?"

"Done it. I told them to deliver the skip for this afternoon. Tomorrow morning I'll finish checking everything and, if you like, I'll make a list of damaged material and material I think needs updating."

"Sounds like a very good idea. At the same time, you could do an inventory."

"Actually, I've already done it. While I was tidying up the materials I made a list of everything."

"Ok, wonderful. By the way, don't forget that next week you're starting your new job as foreman."

"Yes, I've already spoken with a colleague who's going to put me in the picture. I've got loads of questions written down to ask you, to make sure it's all quite clear to me so I can start learning from day one."

"OK, we can take a look at them any time you like."

Dunnit left.

Issjust still didn't get why he was treated so differently.

"Did you see what he's done?"

"Well, he managed to speak to the supervisor and…"

"Yes. But I don't mean just that. It's his ability to surprise you – he's always one step ahead, and does things better than expected. You must realize that, for us managers, who are always worried about things being done properly, the words "done it" are like music to our ears! Efficiency is a breath of fresh air, a relief from stress. And it's not only for other people, it's for yourself. It makes you have a positive attitude towards life and it's good for your self-esteem. Knowing you can say proudly 'I've done what I set out to do,' is an egoboost every time. Do you want me to help you improve?"

"Of course!" said Issjust. "I want to do well, but for some strange reason I don't seem to be doing what my bosses - or I – expect."

"If you want to get ahead, you must concentrate on just one thing."

"Ok, I am prepared to do whatever it takes."

"OK: don't say 'it's just…', ever again. Every time you say it, you're pulling back, and exasperating other people because, when you say that, you are unconsciously focusing on excuses and problems, instead of on action and solutions. It's not good for you, it's bad for your image, and it's exasperating for your bosses."

"Well, I'll try, but it's just that sometimes it's not up to me and …"

* * *
Being able to say "done it" is a breath fresh air
and a relief from stress, both for yourself and for others.
* * *

"No more "it's just"! That's exactly what I meant! You haven't even taken a second to think, and you're already saying "it's just…". If you manage to change this behavior, you'll quickly gain in efficiency and self esteem, and you'll earn professional acknowledgement from others."

"Thank you" said Issjust. "I think your advice is going to be really helpful. Forbidden to say 'it's just…'! But now I'm thinking 'it's just'…"

"There you go again!"

"No, no! I was going to say that I will need to change my name. No more Mr Issjust! From now on, I want to be a member of the Dunnit team. So, as from today, call me Dunn."

"Congratulations! Go for it! And now, remember you have to finish your backlog of work tomorrow – go home."

"Done!"

* * *

Every time you say "it's just….", you unconsciously focus on excuses and problems, instead of action and solutions. It's not good for you, it's bad for your image, and it's exasperating for your bosses.

* * *

CHAPTER . 08

The company's Management Committee was summoned to deal with a problem that would undoubtedly affect the security of its results, and which, even worse, posed a serious problem for the future of the business.

The issue was analysed and discussed at this, and subsequent, meetings, and finally a strategy was laid out to solve the problem and move forward. At this point, the Management Team planned to make some important decisions which would have an impact on most areas of the company. It was then that Antonio asked the burning question:

"How do we sell this idea to our people?"

To Daniel's surprise, the rest of the Senior Managers started to discuss ways to sell the decisions to the team, and they came up with all sort of alternatives:

"We could sound things out, then wait and see how people react, before telling them the whole plan", suggested Marina from the Financial Department.

"We need to decide on an incentive system to help smooth things over, and that will help to compensate. People will get more involved.", pointed out Steve, the Human Resources Director.

"I think it would be better to implement it little by little, as we move forward. If people don't know about the whole plan, they won't get alarmed", added Peter, from Production.

"Well, I think this has to be presented as a management decision, and that's that. The General Director will have to sign a document and we'll tell them that it comes from "the top" and that's all there is to it", said Albert, an old hand in charge of Logistics.

"Perhaps it would simply be enough to put a bit of a "cosmetic gloss" over the scheme. We're all used to giving bad news, so we could find a way to do it without showing the uglier side of it", suggested Michael, from Marketing.

Daniel was speechless. They carried on looking for ways to "sell the plan", as one of them described it. Daniel couldn't believe they had such a bizarre approach to the subject.

At last, David, the General Director, took the chair and said:

"Right. This issue is really important and announcing the plan in the right way is the first step towards its success. I have listened to your various opinions, but I would like to hear Daniel's ideas, as he hasn't told us them yet. Well, how do you think we should sell this to the team?"

Daniel got up and walked around the room. He needed to think before replying. A few seconds later he faced the group and said:

"There is something I don't understand here. Why do we have to "sell" the decision we have made? Aren't we ourselves convinced that this is the right way for us all to move forward? Didn't we all have a part in designing this plan for implementing the changes we need to ensure ourselves a better future?"

He stopped and waited for the answers.

"This is undoubtedly the right thing to do. What's more, I believe that not going ahead with the changes would be irresponsible of us, even if the changes aren't popular," replied Albert.

"It's a necessary plan, *and* it's well structured. It would not only avoid the threat that's affecting us, but it will give the company stability and strength," stated Michael, just before David added:

"We clearly agree that this is the right plan."

One by one, they all agreed. When they had finished, Daniel calmly went on:

"In that case, if we all know and believe that we are doing the right thing, why do we have to "sell" it at all? I don't want to give you a lecture, but I have always thought that, when it comes to decisions, we don't sell them: we simply communicate them. If there is so much to "sell", it means we are not making the right decision and we don't believe in it. In both cases, the problem is not with our teams, but around this table."

Everybody in the room became quiet. Nobody seemed to have the courage to follow Daniel. They looked at each other, waiting for someone else to start.

"Well, that's easy enough to say," said Marina, finally. "But the orders have to be given with great care. I have passed lots of decisions on to my people only to find out later that they didn't understand them, and I'm talking about things that were said officially, not just comments made in the corridor."

"A short while ago, some members of my team came to see me to ask me for the criteria for following something up, and I was amazed! It was all stuff we had already talked about! I agree with Marina, we have to be very careful, because it doesn't matter how many times you say something, people still seem to misunderstand and get confused."

* * *

You don't sell decisions, they simply need to
be communicated properly.

* * *

After this comment from Albert, the General Director said:

"Actually, care has to be taken when transmitting any information, and even more so when you're dealing with delicate strategic issues. That's why I'm worried about what I'm seeing here. I believe we have a very major issue here that we need to improve upon, and it is essential that we tackle it. I would like to deal with it straight away. I learned a lesson long time ago which I should have shared with you: in Management, communication is *not* just saying things."

"I don't quite understand, David," said Michael, a bit puzzled.

"I mean that for a senior manager, for those of us who have accepted the task and challenge of managing people, "Communication" is much more than just saying things; it is making sure that the message you want to convey gets through, and that you achieve the right effect on other people."
"That's clear, and we all agree with you, of course" said Peter quickly.

"No, no," said David. "This is an absolutely essential point, and I want you all to really understand it. What Daniel has said is very valuable. I used to think just like a lot of you do. I was surprised at how difficult some people seemed find it to understand my instructions, my ideas and my messages. Until one day, a great line manager I had helped me to change.

He made me understand that, for every management level, either senior or middle, good communication is one of the fundamental responsibilities. For a good boss it is simply not enough to say 'I've already told you that'. I'm sorry, but that's not good enough.

It is the same as when you hear a number of senior managers saying quite openly: 'I am not very good at communicating - in fact I don't even like it. My strong point is running the business.' They say it perfectly calmly, as if it were no big deal! Can you imagine a bus driver saying "I don't like driving, it's just not my thing"? Don't you think he should be fired on the spot for incompetence? It's exactly the same for us. We need to accept that the position of boss comes with the responsibility of communicating well, and if you're no good at it, you need to improve, urgently!"
Everyone now understood what David was saying. Just like many other managers, they had forgotten one of the basic management tools:

good communication skills, which, at the end of the day, is the only tool they have for relating to their team.

David returned to the original issue, and said to Daniel:

"Daniel, you've always been a good communicator. Not just because you're a talented public speaker, but because of, how shall I put it... your human qualities. Now I understand why your area is always one step ahead in difficult situations. Can you finish explaining to us how you would approach this issue, so we can all learn from your secret?"

"Well," replied Daniel, a little embarrassed "It isn't really a secret. It's just my way of doing things. The key is for me is to believe in the decisions myself, whether they are my own or those of others. I look for the positive side of the decision, because I consider it must have been made for a reason, and I almost always find it.

* * *

Communicating is not just saying things.
The manager is responsible for communicating well.

* * *

After that, everything becomes easier" he added, "because there's nothing to sell. All I have to do is pass the decision on to my people, clearly explaining the reasons. Giving them the same explanations that have convinced me. I've always thought that when we understand why things need to be done, we all get more involved - at least that's what happens to me."

"It sounds ideal. But what if you don't agree with the decision? Sometimes we have to announce something we don't like", Steve pointed out.

"In that case I go to the source of the decision and ask why."

"It's true" remarked Peter, who had been Daniel's boss in the past.

"When you weren't convinced about something, you always used to come and ask me for the reasons behind the decision, without starting to criticize or pretending to look resigned, like other people. And more than once you made me defend and think about my decisions"

He addressed the group:

"I even had to rectify once, because when I tried to explain my decision to him I realized that I was putting my foot in it!"

"In any case," continued Daniel, "sometimes it's not a question of liking a decision or not. I've learned to take on board decisions I don't like, because everyone has his or her own point of view and preferences, and it's impossible to like everybody's ideas. When that happens, I concentrate on working out if the decision adds any value, and if it is coherent or not, because the person who decides is entitled to choose their own option. If I believe the decision is a valid alternative, and even if I think there are better ones, I support it, look for its good points, and pass it on without making things more complicated."

Some of his colleagues started to applaud Daniel, and the rest followed suit. Despite their individual limitations, as a group they were prepared to learn, and Marina finished by saying:

"Well, I think we've made major progress on this management team today. This is the sort of thing we need in order to learn quickly. Thanks, Daniel, and thank you, David. I propose we review all the good things that this ambitious and exciting plan we have designed is about to bring. And then we communicate it to everybody in the same way, with the same enthusiasm we feel ourselves. What do you think David?"

"That's the way to talk, Marina. Let's get going!"

* * *

When people understand why things have to be done,
they get more involved and work better.

* * *

PART TWO

The two commitments needed
in order to make a change

After the above reflections, it's time to get on with it. Each one to his or her oar! The managers have to get on and manage well, and the workers have to be well-enough managed to get on with performing well.

The combination of these two commitments can change things to an amazing degree; together, they can generate an overwhelming energy, and create a new professional environment that enables people to face the Great Challenge with every chance of success.

CHAPTER . 09

The First Commitment

For those who manage:
Commit yourself to people's RIGHT to be managed properly.

Here in the 21st century, people should have enough knowledge and data for shareholders, staff, and society in general to know who we are entrusting with our money or our work. It is our "right" as shareholders, managers, and workers, to expect our companies to be well managed.

The question is: How do we know when a company is being well managed? How do we separate the wheat from the chaff? And how does one measure the quality of a company's management team? We see plenty of information in financial reports and balance sheets, but it is mainly of a financial nature.

The trouble is, this information often gives no indication of the standard of the management. This information is necessary, but it not sufficient, as it lacks an equally vital point: a serious analysis of the quality of the senior management. The shareholders, managers and staff are entitled to expect their company to be well managed.

This kind of analysis should appear in the Audit Reports and Company Reports, for the simple reason that companies can't function on their own. They function as a result of the decisions and managerial methods of the senior management team. That's why it is essential to incorporate this information today. The shareholders of any company, simply *because they are shareholders*, are entitled to expect the company to be managed well. The entire staff, the people who devote their efforts and talent to keeping a stable job and producing satisfactory company results, are equally entitled to expect this.

At the end of the day, when a company is not well managed, the first ones to pay the price are the workers and shareholders. We have recently seen glaring examples of this in major international companies. Nowadays, no leading corporations ever fail clearly to establish their mission, their vision and their values.

With these transcendental missions of theirs, the main thing for the company is to maintain the interest of its shareholders through its results, and hence, its long-term operation. It is therefore essential to make a job in that company interesting to top-quality professionals, as they are the ones who will take the company forward. A well-run company well means a good quality management team. But, what is quality management?

Quality management is the ideal management of the resources and features that make up the company. This means material and financial resources, information, and, of course, people.

If information, risks, strategy, decisions, material resources and people are not managed correctly failure, and all its consequences, are just a matter of time.

Here's a curious fact: Approximately 99% of the companies that fail do so due to bad global management, lack of vision of the future, and wrong decisions.
The other 1% were just plain unlucky.

It is hard enough coping with changes in the market and competitors' strategies without the adding to this brew other factors that *can* be controlled, such as good or bad management.

For decades, we have been discussing the importance of people in the corporate mechanism. Perhaps it's about time that all this talk was turned into a right: the right to good management. The truth is that a company is like a "machine" in which people are one of the cogwheels. It's not just a matter of personal values. You can manage by either involving people, or by using them. These two styles of management have the same verb tense, but completely different

51

meanings.

Nowadays, there are lots of companies in which the general management is not directly responsible for the standard of people management, and in which the IT department has more resources, a bigger budget and more strategic importance than Human Resources.

And yet, the most perfect, powerful and amazing computer on earth is the human brain. What a waste!

The corporate graveyards are full of companies buried by bad decisions, or by their inability to make decisions during a particular process.

These are decisions that have to be made by senior management. If we don't want to become extinct, we have to demand quality management. Also, if wrong decisions are standard practice, we should at least be told about it in time.

It has become common for managers of dubious (and even appallingly low) efficiency, to move from one job to another, leaving behind them a toxic trail of corporate asphyxia, beautifully wrapped in spectacular short-term figures.
So, how do we measure management quality?
We should have a quantifiable scale that takes into account both results and future prospects when judging the reliability of a company.

It is hard enough to achieve success with all the usual market setbacks and competitors' strategies. There is no need to add a factor of risk that can be avoided, i.e.: bad managerial action.

Audit Reports should include the turnover of qualified managers and staff. This is one of the best ways to assess the quality of management. When the talent leaves a company, it is because something is going wrong. We have seen it thousands of times, and probably experienced it personally: when the senior managers insist on taking the wrong path, they end up alone or, even worse, blindly followed by those who are unable to speak up.

Another interesting piece of information is the average age of staff and the rate of staff rejuvenation, together with early retirement policies.

A company that pre-retires staff systematically at specific age runs the risk of wasting huge quantities of talent and experience. The reason for doing this is that it is cheaper to replace these people with trainees, which is good for the immediate short-term accounts, but cyanide for the future.

Ideally, a history of the results of strategic decisions taken in previous years should be added to the Annual Report, in order to gauge the level of correct decisions and failures.

Of course, this data could always be glossed over somehow, in which case information that is hard to manipulate and which provides revealing conclusions could be added, such as surveys on the internal prestige of the senior managers of the work environment.

When companies have good projects and are well managed, this is noticeable even in the corridors.

* * *

You can manage by either involving people or by using them.
It is not possible for the majority of staff to be useless,
but it is possible for some of them to lose their enthusiasm
for work to the point where they appear to be useless.

* * *

A burnt-out, pessimistic and negative member of staff is another unmistakable symptom of mediocre management.

It is not possible for 90 % of the staff to be useless. It is possible to have a few who discourage and de-motivate the rest, until they move on…

In short: nowadays, it should be compulsory practice to provide an analysis that is reliable enough to be used to decide whether or not to back a management team. The right to be managed properly means that good quality management of people, resources, and decisions are all a requirement. Good management usually reaps huge profits for employees, shareholders and society. Bad management gives people too many problems, at least in financial terms.

At the beginning of 2002, the employees of an American corporate giant began to sue their management, accusing them of getting rich at the shareholders' and workers' expense. Perhaps this was to be the first step towards a new system. This is just one example of the consequences of managing well or badly.

From these pages, and for all of the above reasons, I hereby claim our right to have well-managed companies, along with our right to control these companies via accessible, reliable and easy-to-understand data and indexes.

I therefore encourage you to make the first real, essential commitment to making change possible: as either middle-, or senior-level managers, we must commit to dealing with our direct and indirect collaborators with a high managerial standard, both inside and outside our own corporate environment.

CHAPTER . 10

The Second Commitment

For those who are well managed: Commit to the RIGHT to perform well.

The great challenge of improving our lives and work will never be feasible if the first commitment is not accompanied by second one.

It is now up to the workers, and even the trade unions, who represent a large and fundamental part of the company. But not under present terms. We need to re-focus the workers' and the trade unions' commitment, with a view to improving the quality of working life.

The workers and trade unions should be the first to naturally reprimand an underperforming worker, to exclude those that don't perform their duties, those that cause damage, those that deceive their colleagues and the company by clocking in for absent colleagues or exceeding their break periods (breakfast, lunch, coffee breaks, etc.), causing a decline in their performance as a group.

If the workers would add care and commitment to the quality of their work to their internal rules, and if they would get more involved with securing the profits of the company, these profits would reach previously unheard-of dimensions.

They would receive such massive support from all sides, including the management, that they could change the world, achieve trade union goals that are today unimaginable, and truly help to create a better business environment, and, as a result, a better place to live for everyone - both for those who work and for those who live with those who work.

Only with this kind of approach can we tackle areas that are still in need of improvement, such as coherent working hours for parents; real flexibility that enables people to work and cope with the personal needs that crop up throughout our lives; demanding a better standard of management from our bosses; the moral and human strength to negotiate collective agreements; new types of contracts that would prioritize good performance rather than mere physical presence at work.

Our colleagues and the trade unions are there to protect workers, and that shouldn't just mean anyone on the payroll, but those who perform well, the real workers who, as long they are managed properly, will feel committed to the company.

Their role is to maintain standards at work, in every context, not to serve as protection for the mediocre. They must be the first to take serious action against disloyal workers who have no commitment to quality at work, and who betray their own colleagues with their absences, causing disorganisation, a negative environment and, even worse, a decline in the moral strength to fight for new improvements and rights. The lazy and mediocre must not be accepted by, and hidden amongst, staff who *do* **work and perform, nor within the trade unions.**

Workers who undertake to perform well in exchange for due attention to their demands will have a better place in the new system, and this will be apparent in trade unions, staff, and the lower-, middle-, and senior-level management, because they will defend areas of common interest and because the only enemies to beat will be bad behavior and injustice.

* * *

The enemies to be beaten, both for decision-makers
and those who perform, are bad behavior and injustice,
regardless of who does the work
and who is paying for it.

* * *

In the new working world, when someone is not performing efficiently, a distinction has to be made between those who don't know how, those who are unable, and those who just don't want to.

The first group can be given the training they need; the second can be offered the support they need; and the last, those who don't want to reach the required level, will have to be removed, whoever they are, and whatever their position in the structure.

It's a matter of equilibrium, harmony and common sense, associated with a commitment to doing well and working hard and to a high standard. A matter of taking on board the fact that the lack of good management at the senior levels is just as unacceptable as shirking off work at the lower levels, and pointing the finger at a manager who mismanages in the same way as at an employee who adds little or no value.

It is about everybody cooperating within, and for the benefit of, this new system; about working shoulder to shoulder in order to achieve high standards, and about safeguarding this encouraging new environment. Workers who are unsuitable, either at management or staff level, should be removed from their jobs without a second thought, making way for others. They should be censured by everybody: clients, shareholders, trade unionists, senior management and staff. Perhaps they could then meditate on how difficult it is to maintain the balance between decent, secure jobs and the profits required in order to provide such jobs.

* * *

Equilibrium, harmony and common sense are possible.
It is about ensuring there is a commitment to working
to a high standard, and that poor workers, professionals,
line managers or collaborators, surrender their jobs
to those who contribute and add value to the company.
* * *

Therefore, I claim the "right" of businesspeople and managers who are dedicated to their teams, and who practice good management, and the right of all workers, to expect and achieve the high-level of performance we all need in order to survive and progress.

CHAPTER . 11

The Great Challenge

Making work and life compatible with quality.

Who invented this great deception? How did we get ourselves into this absurd situation? Work, work, work - we live to work. From Monday to Friday, our life passes us by on tiptoes, as we are completely absorbed by our working days, and we end up trying to get our breath back on the weekend.

That's enough! It's time to rebel and put things back where they belong. The greatest fraud that we can commit against Nature is to waste such a large part of our life – especially considering how short it is! Being unable to enjoy life because we don't know how to work better is so utterly ridiculous that it makes us unworthy of being known as "intelligent creatures".

* * *

Considering how short life is, being unable to enjoy it
because we don't know how to work better, is utterly ridiculous.

* * *

When work accumulates and there are financial difficulties, the solution is not to work longer hours or inject more money. That will only delay the problem temporarily. The solution is to be creative and do things differently. When we have problems or a big workload, we must work better, not more.

In a survey carried out by Otto Walter in 2002, on "What do bosses expect from their staff?", it turned out that 96.7 % of managers and senior managers don't think workers being willing to work longer hours is a fundamental asset. In fact, 77.53% of them highlighted this as one of the lowest factors of importance on the scale, in terms of what they expect from staff.

If we managers don't value office presence, if, in fact, we are actually the first to be sick of such slavery; if, out in the street, we can hear the voices calling for a balance between work and family life balance, or personal life and professional life; if we all agree on this, then what on earth are we waiting for?

There is only one priority that determines all of this. More than 97 % of managers consider it very important or essential that their employees should "fulfill their duties", "show interest in their jobs", "be honest and cooperative", "be efficient", " work as part of a team", "disagree and offer alternatives" and "ask questions without fear".

* * *

When there are problems, or a big workload,
we must work better, not more.

* * *

If all of this is taken on board by everyone, from the top down, change will be possible.

It is no good saying "the company" expects too many things that are not possible. Who is the "company"? Does "the company" talk and think by itself? The shareholders do not expect people to be exploited; they only expect a return on their capital. The two are not necessarily connected, if managed properly. In fact, quite the opposite: if the job is done properly, in a good environment, with the right working hours and rhythm, with managers setting coherent working rules so that staff also enjoy a reasonable quality of life, while creating a positive and demanding working environment, then productivity will increase and profits will multiply.

Every employee who does his or her job correctly should be treated well by the company, live a professional and private life of quality, and enjoy time with his or her family, and this is as it should be. Working overtime should actually be considered a bad habit.

Overtime means that there is either is too much work - which means it needs prioritizing and that help should be found - or that things are not being done properly. In both cases, action should be taken, but this doesn't mean working longer hours.

If people want to stay in the office after office hours, because they enjoy their jobs, or because their personal ambition makes them do it, or simply because they don't want to go home, that's up to them. But they should not expect everybody else to join them, or expect extra recognition. It is not a matter of controlling when staff clock in or out, but controlling *how* they perform.

Managers who work 10 or 11 hours a day – and there are many – ought to counterbalance this with days off, so they can rest, as they must. Of course, all of this is only possible if everybody undertakes to safeguard the essential values agreed within the company, and to work hard and to a high standard. In fact, anybody who jeopardizes this equilibrium by not keeping in line with these values should be removed from the team without delay.

A good idea, in larger companies, might be to create the job of Head of Working Standards: a person or department given the necessary authority, in charge of supervising the standard of work in all contexts. For example, a boss who often arranges meetings outside normal office hours - behavior that should actually be reprimanded, if it is repeated – is a case that should be treated as a serious fault, on a par with absenteeism or disloyalty.

One-off situations are one thing; when they become standard practice, it is quite another. If some workers show low performance levels, or spend too long on coffee or cigarette breaks or lunch, they should also be reprimanded because this can jeopardize the overall stable environment. If a department tends to work beyond official office hours with no justification, it should be restructured, because this is a clear symptom that is not working correctly, either because of an excessive workload, or a low standard of work.

Managers should impose time limits. We have endless working days, to which we have to add travel time. We should not allow ourselves stay in the office beyond a sensible time. We need to help each other to be strict about this, because we keep on falling into the trap of wanting everything done immediately.

If we make it a rule to leave the workstation at a set hour, we will soon change our working habits and the way we prioritize and distribute our tasks. This is the only way we will learn to work better.

* * *
We keep falling into the trap
of wanting everything done immediately.
We want to, and must, work well, in order to perform and live well.
* * *

There is another universal deception. With the arrival of new technologies, it was predicted that we would achieve much more, productivity would shoot up, everything would get better and we would work less. What has actually happened? It is true that technology enables us to do more things and to increase productivity, but it has been used to cut the number of jobs.

Therefore, we don't do more – we do the same but with fewer people!

Before, we used to receive a fax or a letter and had a few days to study the issue and respond. Now we receive an e-mail, and are expected to reply straight away.

Before, when traveling to see a client, we used to have hours to think, reflect, create, or organize things. Nowadays, those minutes are filled up with calls on the mobile phone. There isn't a break. We no longer own our time: anyone is free to steal it.

That's enough! We are sick of spending our lives working the wrong way! We want to work the right way, in order to both perform and live well! It's about time we changed this working world of ours – it's a world that doesn't make sense anymore.

We have to stop rewarding presence over efficiency! Some of the most developed countries in the world are the most inflexible in such matters. All of them are committed to working hard and to a high standard and, in exchange, everyone can go home on time, no problem.

It works!!

* * *

Let's stop rewarding presence over efficiency!
* * *

We are talking about some of the most powerful economies in the world. What are we waiting for to join the first division? If you call these companies at ten past five in the afternoon, nobody's there - not even the senior managers. But during working hours they deliver maximum performance, and this means everybody gains something: the shareholders see the profits from a job well done; the managers see their teams' high performance and reliability; the workers have labor agreements that offer them a more balanced life; and the company survives and grows.

There is a lot of talk on this subject, but we don't seem to make any conclusive decisions. If we accept the results of the survey, and the backing of 97% of management-level staff, then maybe it's time to take action and provide a new working framework; time we fought to get rid of this nonsense for once and for all. It is so deep-rooted that it is destroying our quality of life.

I know I am just a humble oarsman, but I want to be able to say to myself "I did what I could". Therefore, on my own behalf and on behalf of all those who have the will to change the present system, I propose, and accept, the following "commandments" or "values":

Commitment To Change

I
As a Shareholder,

I promise to fight to secure good quality management, and to respect workers who perform well, in those companies in which i have shares, and even at the expense of part of my own short-term profits.

II
As a Businessperson,

I promise that all employees who fulfill their working duties to a good standard within office hours can go home.
On time, according to the agreed schedule for their professional level.

III
As a Manager,

I promise to promote the culture of prioritizing eficiency over presence, and to train my team so that they can learn to do their jobs well, and go home on time.

IV
As an Employee,

I promise to do my utmost every day, participating in a positive, proactive and productive climate that will produce profits, so that decent jobs are assured, and so all of us who do our work properly may be able to work and live with quality.

We are putting our lives and our families on the line here.

Why do we have children if we can't watch them grow up?
Why seven days a week if we don't know how to live them?

I am excited to see the new trends and waves of opinion that support this new system, and I have decided to start putting these values into practice in my own working environment. Because in the end, it's all about making THE GREAT CHALLENGE possible: quality of work and life.

Do you like the idea? Come on, then. Each man to his oar.

* * *

The Great Challenge:
LET'S MAKE IT POSSIBLE, AMONG ALL OF US:
QUALITY OF WORK AND LIFE
* * *

Epilogue

This last story was born one night when my nine-year-old daughter asked me to tell her a story in which the main character was a pen. So, I began the story, and it took on a form, and ended with an idea, that could apply equally well to the business world.

When I finished telling her the story, I went straight to the computer and started typing the story, to get deeper into its ideas.

This is the result, which I offer you as a small gift from my daughter, Nina.

The Pen That Couldn't Write

Once upon the time there was a pen that couldn't write. It lived with its friends in a pencil case. It was often chosen, but then put back into the case with a disappointed exclamation:

"This pen doesn't write!"

The pen was frightened, not only because the rest of the pens talked about it, but also because, one of these days, it was going to end up in the garbage bin.

It sensed that next time it wouldn't be so lucky as to be put back in the pencil case. Next time might be the end.

The rest of the pens called it the "odd one out", because it didn't know how to write and, perhaps, because of its unusual design, and because it didn't boast about anything and, of course, it had a different way of seeing things.

The red pen always talked about how wonderful his bright line was, which could be seen from a long way away. The yellow and green highlighters boasted:

"We are only used for highlighting the most important things". They were all pompous and arrogant.

The plain blue ballpoint was proud of being indispensable, and its cousin the serious Mont Blanc fountain pen, preferred to keep its distance from everybody else, like an aristocrat, just because, as it used to say:

"They only use *me* to sign checks".

It was actually very elegant, but a bit stuck up, so nobody much liked it.

The pencil was a nice guy, always ready to do things, but his hobby was arguing with the eraser:

"I don't know why you always have to interfere with what I write. Who are you to erase what I do?"

And the eraser would take the bait and respond:

"I only remove what you do *wrong*. Learn to write without making mistakes, clever clogs!".

They always went on like this, but they didn't know that, deep down, they were really very fond of each other.

One day, the owner of the pencil case opened it up and chose the "odd one out".

"Right. This is it", thought the pen with resignation.

Sure enough, when the owner started to write he immediately moaned:

"Here we go again! I picked this pen again! I'm fed up with it."

Somebody standing next to him said,

"Give it to me", and tried to write with it. It didn't last five seconds.

"It doesn't work. I'll throw it away".

The pen felt depressed. She knew it: the time had come.

Nevertheless, before she was put in the garbage bin, the owner's little daughter said:

"Daddy, give it to me. I like it!"

Her father smiled and gave it to her. Why did she want it if it didn't work? He thought she probably liked its unusual shape.

A few minutes later, the girl cried out, "Hey, look how pretty this looks!.

The girl had in her hands a piece of navy blue cardboard, and showed it to her father: "Look daddy, look how pretty!"

"Hey, look at that, David. Doesn't it look good?" The father passed the cardboard to his friend, who was very impressed:

"Wow, it is a white pen! The white ink looks great on a dark surface. I've never seen a pen like this."

"Listen, we could use it to write Christmas cards. This year we bought Christmas cards on dark paper, and would look really great if we wrote and signed them with this".
"Good idea! Let's do that!" answered his friend.

"I am a white pen!" thought the pen. "It looked as if I couldn't write. But it just so happens I'm super special - and what's more, I'm going to write the Christmas cards! I can't believe it!"

Her owner put her gently back in the pencil case, but this time he made sure to put her in a special place. He took the ruler out of its usual place to put the fantastic pen there, in the special place she deserved. Of course, the ruler, square and strict as ever, kept complaining:

"Hey, that's my place! It's not fair, that's the place for rulers, and always has been!"

The "odd one out" felt very happy now, and told everyone about the discovery. And her friends were very happy for her. (Everyone except the highlighters, of course, because when the pen told them about the Christmas cards, they went yellow with envy!).

* * *

Certain exceptional people end up going unnoticed
because nobody wants to discover if, inside that unusual person,
there might be a valuable and special skill.

* * *

Sometimes in a company one meets "odd" people, who, like the white pen, simply have some very special and unusual skills and approaches. That's why they often end up going unnoticed or getting left out - just because nobody wants to find out whether, hidden behind their unusualness, there might be a different way of doing things that might turn out to be incredibly useful for certain tasks that "normal" people can't handle.

These "odd ones out" can usually be identified because they are people who are very involved in the company, who question what is done wrong, and are very interested in doing things right.

They are always ready to improve and add their best, to commit themselves. But they are not always the best at doing their current tasks, and may even be a nuisance to their bosses.

Don't be mistaken, though! A conflictive person is not the same as a white pen: the former don't like working, the latter love having goals. It is a matter of finding the right place for them: special tasks require special people.

Perhaps you yourself were once a white pen that many bosses did not appreciate - and today you are a successful professional.

* * *

A conflictive person is not the same as a brave
and special professional:
the former don't like working, the latter love having goals.

* * *

In fact, you were the "odd one out" among ordinary staff, just because you had the makings of a leader: because you were unafraid to get involved in complicated tasks, to provide solutions that nobody listened to, or because you didn't just swallow what you were told. A mediocre person sees these things as insolence, or failure to adapt. Discover your "white pens" and you will find an elite group who will reinforce the team and give you scope for the future.

Don't reject the "odd ones out" just because they are different. Analyze their oddness and maybe just one of the unsettled sheep may turn out to be a potential champion, lost and disorientated among the docile flock. To distinguish them from the rest, give them an important goal, accept some of their suggestions and let them lead a project.

If they can do it and prove their value by doing an excellent job, you will have found a valuable and authentic leader. You may have just found your best collaborator.

And now all they need is to be managed with the quality that they deserve.

* * *

Sometimes we find the best collaborators
among the lively and restless.
They only need to be managed with the quality they deserve.

* * *

70

AN EXTRA CHAPTER

What to do for starters

When my editor read the manuscript of this book, he was the first to ask me for a practical tool to help him find a starting point. He was eager to "go there …".

An important point is to find out if, depending on your position, you are a boss who manages well or a high-performance collaborator.

In short, it is about checking the professional standard of each individual. How do we know the standard of quality of a director or a collaborator is correct?
There are several techniques for measuring the quality of professional performance: assessment of duties, surveys on the working environment, analysis of individual results, etc. But the most reliable systems tend to be the most complex ones in terms of the effort involved in implementing them and the subsequent analysis of data.

I therefore propose a very simple and efficient system. It is based on something one learns with experience: professionals who are highly valued by those who work alongside them always end up being the most efficient, reliable, productive and positive ones. And good mangers tend to be those who show higher overall results in terms of competence, and those who have above-average added value and results.

So, why complicate things? Let's measure those very things: it will enable us to quickly and simply identify the good managers and the best professionals in the company. If we add to this an assessment of the results obtained by that person over the last two or three years, the system becomes almost unfailingly accurate. So, if someone has a satisfactory track record in terms of results and, in addition, has earned the respect and professional appreciation of those around him or her, we will be looking at an excellent team member, either as a boss or as a collaborator.

Try it on your own team. Start with yourself, even. It's just a matter of asking some questions about the people around you and checking their professional or managerial quality. On the next page you will find a test to complete.

Make copies of these questions and give them to the people working with you. Ask them to answer the questions honestly. They must remain anonymous, which is why they only need to CIRCLE THEIR ANSWERS. When they finish, they can put the answers in a box or an envelope. That way nobody will know who answered what.

The higher the response is, the more realistic the result will be (a minimum of four evaluators is recommended). If there is currently an ongoing conflict with somebody, it is better to exclude this person from the test, as it will distort the results.

Go ahead and give it a go. Expect from yourself what you expect from others. I trust that, whatever the outcome, the conclusions you come to will be useful and for the better.

PROFESSIONAL QUALITY TEST

This test is to assess (NAME)   ....

	A	**B**	**C**
If you had your own company, and were thinking of hiring a good new professional, would you employ this person without a second thought?	YES	MAYBE	NO
Do you think this person's contribution and presence is of use to the team? Are they helpful, and do they contribute to making things better?	YES	AVERAGE	NO
If you were able to choose between continuing to work with this person or bringing in somebody new and unknown, would you rather carry on with the first person?	YES	I WOULD'T MIND EITHER WAY	NO
Is this person competent and reliable?	YES	ONLY SOMETIMES	NO
Would you say this person is involved with the company's goals and that they convey enthusiasm?	YES	AVERAGE	NO
This person is exemplary and is concerned with the excellence and quality of work.	YES	AVERAGE	NO
If you were no longer working for this company, and a good friend from another company called you for references on this person, would you recommend this person as a professional?	YES	THEY'RE NEITHER GOOD NOR BAD	NO

RESULTS

Add up the points according to the following scale:

A=2 points
B=1 point
C=0 point

13 or 14 points: You can be satisfied, your level of professional quality is excellent.

12 points: Just passed, you need to improve without delay.

Less than 12 points: You have not reached the professional standard that everyone is expecting of you and of which you are most certainly capable. I recommend that you talk and listen to people, and ask for and accept help in order to improve. You need to be prepared to make improvements on certain necessary aspects. Go for it!

FAREWELL

I would like to end by encouraging everyone to decide to "go there", to take a step towards finding the new balance between work and personal life.

It's not just a question of finding the right moment, or the right people doing the right thing, above and below you.

It's about each of us individually undertaking to live and work better. If we all do our share, and are committed, the great challenge won't be a mere Utopia, but a real objective.

Every one of us must do their utmost - that way we will soon see some rewarding results:

Quality of work and life

I hope you have enjoyed reading this book, and I trust I have awoken the urge to get going. I would be delighted to hear your comments and opinions. You can send them to the following e-mail address : rema@ottowalter.com

Paco Muro

The End of this book - and The Beginning of action.

Each man to his oar!

Visit our website:
www.empresaactiva.com

www.ingramcontent.com/pod-product-compliance
Lightning Source LLC
Chambersburg PA
CBHW031952190326
41519CB00007B/777